LEVEL
1

Frogs

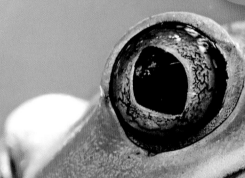

Elizabeth Carney

NATIONAL
GEOGRAPHIC

Washington, D.C.

For my parents, Marty and Cindy Carney, who charitably endured my collections of slimy creatures. —E.C.

Published by National Geographic Partners, LLC, Washington, DC 20036.

Library of Congress Cataloging-in-Publication Data
Carney, Elizabeth, 1981-
Frogs! / by Elizabeth Carney.
p. cm. -- (National Geographic readers)
ISBN 978-1-4263-0392-0 (pbk. : alk. paper) -- ISBN 978-1-4263-0393-7 (hardcover : alk. paper)
1. Frogs--Juvenile literature. I. Title.
QL668.E2C346 2009
597.8'9--dc22
20080140281

GI = Getty Images; MP = Minden Pictures; NGIC = National Geographic Image Collection; SS = Shutterstock
Cover, Digital Vision; 1, SS; 2, Michael & Patricia Fogden/MP; 4-5, Michael Durham/MP; 6 (UP), Roger Wilmshurst/Frank Lane Picture Agency; 6 (LO), Pete Oxford/MP; 7 (LE), Joe McDonald/GI; 7 (RT), Gallo Images/age fotostock; 8, Norbert Wu/Superstock; 9, Gerald Lopez/Associated Press; 10-11, Mark Moffett/MP; 12, Visuals Unlimited; 13 (UP), Pete Oxford/Nature Picture Library; 13 (LO), Jupiterimages/Getty Images; 14, SmileStudio/SS; 14-15, Buddy Mays/Alamy Stock Photo; 16, Steve Winter/NGIC; 17, Mark Moffett/MP; 18 (UP), Michael & Patricia Fogden/MP/GI; 18 (LO), Michael Lustbader/Science Source; 19 (UP), Christian Ziegler/Danita Delimont Agency; 19 (LO), Digital Vision; 20-21, Jupiter Images/GI; 21 (UP), Pete Oxford/MP; 21 (LO), Juniors Bildarchiv GmbH/Alamy Stock Photo; 22-23, Glow Images/GI; 24, Christian Ziegler; 25, Robert Clay/Alamy Stock Photo; 26 (LE), Paula Gallon; 26 (RT), Michael & Patricia Fogden/MP; 27 (LE), Dr. Morley Read/SS; 27 (RT), Carol Wien/Mira Images; 28, Don Farrall/Photodisc/GI; 29, Dorling Kindersley/GI; 30 (UP), Geoff Brightling/Dorling Kindersley; 30 (LE), Michael & Patricia Fogden/MP; 31 (UP, BOTH), Joel Sartore/National Geographic Photo Ark/NGIC; 31 (LO), David A. Northcott/Corbis Documentary/GI; 32 (UP LE), Gerald Lopez/Associated Press; 32 (UP RT), Paula Gallon; 32 (LO LE), Gallo Images/age fotostock; 32 (LO RT), Due Daly/Nature Picture Library

Collection copyright © 2023 National Geographic Partners, LLC
Collection ISBN (paperback): 978-1-4263-7683-2
Collection ISBN (library edition): 978-1-4263-7686-3

Printed in South Korea
23/ISK/1

Table of Contents

Splash!

Pacific Chorus Frog

Q What happened to the frog's car when it broke down?

A It got toad.

Splish, splash.
What is that sound?
What is hopping and
jumping around?
What loves to swim?
What loves to eat bugs?
It's a frog!
Can you hop like a frog?

Frogs live all over the world, except Antarctica. Frogs usually live in wet places. They like rivers, lakes, and ponds.

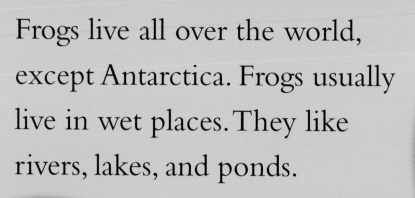

Marsh Frog

Andean Marsupial Frog

Antarctica is the continent at the South Pole.

Habitat: The natural place where a plant or animal lives

Red—Eyed Tree Frog

Bullfrog

But some frogs live in trees. Some even live in the desert. Frogs can be found all over the world. Wherever they live, that's their habitat.

Croak!

Look at this frog croaking! Some frogs' throats puff up when they make sounds. Each type of frog makes its own sound.

Lake Frog

Coqui Frog

Ribbit!

Croak: The deep, hoarse noise that a frog makes

The coqui frog is named after the sound it makes. It sounds like "CO-KEE!" This frog is the size of a quarter. Even small frogs can make loud noises.

Frogs make different sounds
for different reasons. Sometimes
it's to warn other frogs of
danger. Sometimes it's to call
to frogs nearby.

Dancing Frog

This frog lives around noisy waterfalls. Other frogs would not be able to hear its calls. So it dances instead! It sticks out one leg, and then the other. Can you dance like this frog?

Frog Food

What is a frog's favorite food? Usually it's insects. Frogs eat dragonflies and crickets and other bugs.

Green Frog

Q Why are frogs so happy?

A They eat what bugs them!

Amazon Horned Frog

Some frogs eat bigger animals like worms and mice. The American bullfrog even eats other frogs!

American Bullfrog

13

What's that pink flash? It's how a frog catches bugs. It shoots out its long, sticky tongue at a passing bug. The frog pulls the bug into its mouth.

If your tongue were as long as a frog's, it would reach to your belly button!

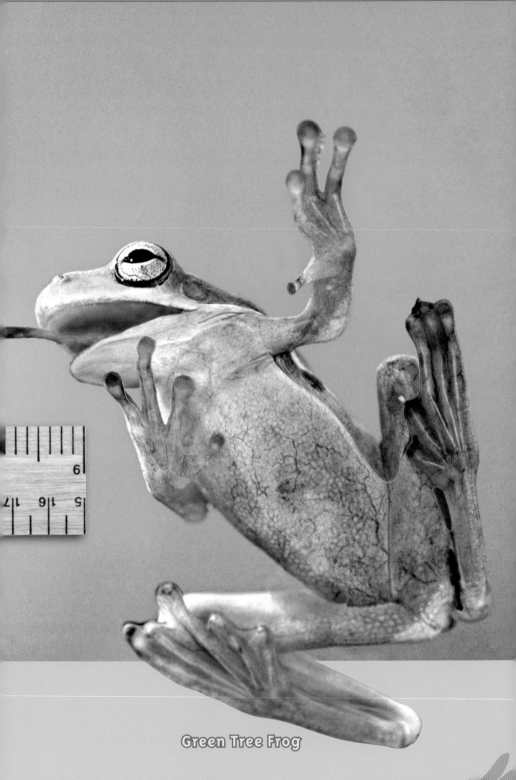

Green Tree Frog

Every Size and Color

Frogs can be many different sizes.

Microfrog

The smallest frog is as big as a fingernail.
The largest is as big as a rabbit.

Goliath Frog

Frogs can be different colors, too.

Tiger Striped Leaf Frog

Some are green or brown.

Amazonian Poison Dart Frog

Others have stripes or spots.

Red Poison Dart Frog

Frogs can be red, yellow, or orange.

Blue Poison Dart Frog

They can even be bright blue!

Watch Out!

These colorful frogs may look pretty. But watch out! These frogs have poison in their skin. Their bright color warns enemies not to eat them.

Poison Dart Frog

Ribbit!

Poison:
Something that can kill or hurt living things

Poison Dart Frog

Yellow Banded Poison Dart Frog

This little frog is only an inch long. Its name is Terribilis, which means "the terrible one." How did it get this name? By being the most deadly frog of all! One Terribilis has enough poison to kill 20,000 mice.

Terribilis

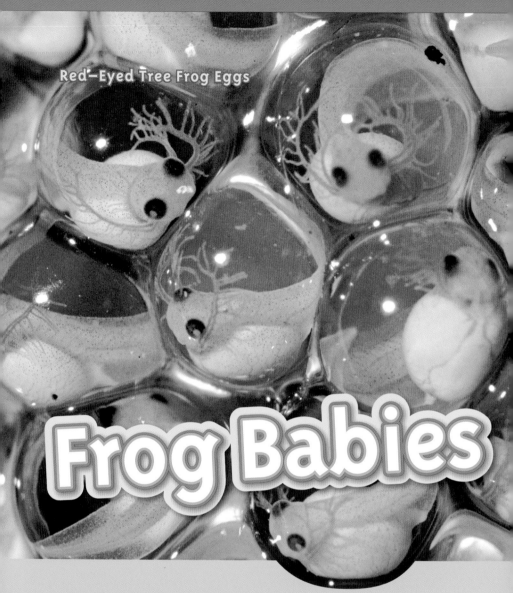

Red-Eyed Tree Frog Eggs

Frog Babies

All frogs, even the Terribilis, have mothers. Mother frogs lay eggs. When the eggs are ready, out pop the tadpoles!

Tadpoles are baby frogs. But they don't look like frogs yet. Tadpoles have tails. They live only in water.

Pacific Tree Frog Tadpole

Tadpoles grow up to be frogs.

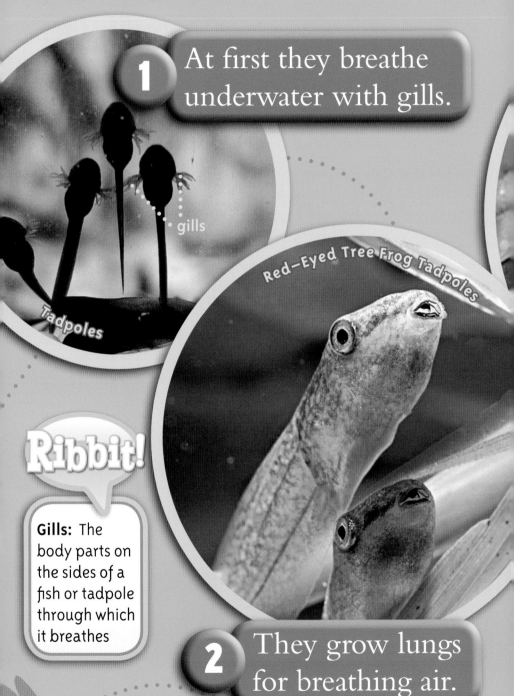

1 At first they breathe underwater with gills.

gills

Tadpoles

Red-Eyed Tree Frog Tadpoles

Ribbit!

Gills: The body parts on the sides of a fish or tadpole through which it breathes

2 They grow lungs for breathing air.

3 They grow legs for hopping and swimming.

Monkey Frog Tadpole

4 In three months, they lose their tails.

Bullfrog

It's time to hop out of the water!

Toads Are Frogs, Too!

What's the difference between toads and frogs?

FROG

Some frogs are poisonous.

Moist and smooth

Teeth in upper jaw

Long, powerful jumping legs; most frogs have webbed hind feet.

Eggs laid in clusters, or groups

Toads are a type of frog. Frogs spend most of their lives around water. Toads spend more time on dry land. Their bodies are built for where they live.

TOAD

Eyes do not bulge out from the body; a poison gland is located behind each eye.

Dry and bumpy

No teeth

Eggs laid in long chains (but a few toads give birth to live young)

Shorter legs (for walking)

SUPER FROGS!

TWO FACED FAKER

A FAKE FACE FOOLS ENEMIES WHEN THIS FROG TURNS AROUND!

TWO HEADS....

...ARE BETTER THAN ONE!!

The HIGH FLYER

WHOOSH!

IT'S A BIRD, IT'S A PLANE!

It's a Gliding Leaf Frog!

ANY FROG CAN JUMP, BUT WATCH ME GLIDE!

gills

CROAK
The deep, hoarse noise that a frog makes

GILLS
The body parts on the sides of a fish or tadpole through which it breathes

HABITAT
The natural place where a plant or animal lives

POISON
Something that can kill or hurt living things

NATIONAL
GEOGRAPHIC

Washington, D.C.

To Arya, welcome to the world! —M.Q.

Published by National Geographic Partners, LLC, Washington, DC 20036.

Designed by Yay! Design

The author and publisher gratefully acknowledge the expert content review of this book by Mike McClure, general curator, the Maryland Zoo, and J. Jill Heatley, associate professor, Department of Small Animal Clinical Sciences, College of Veterinary Medicine & Biomedical Sciences, Texas A&M University, and the literacy review of this book by Mariam Jean Dreher, professor of reading education, University of Maryland, College Park.

Library of Congress Cataloging-in-Publication Data

Names: Quattlebaum, Mary, author.
Title: Hedgehogs / Mary Quattlebaum.
Description: Washington, DC: National Geographic Kids, 2020. | Series: National geographic readers | Audience: Ages 4-6 | Audience: Grades K-1
Identifiers: LCCN 2019051448 (print) | LCCN 2019051449 (ebook) | ISBN 9781426338304 (paperback) | ISBN 9781426338311 (library binding) | ISBN 9781426338328 (ebook) | ISBN 9781426338335 (ebook other)
Subjects: LCSH: Hedgehogs--Juvenile literature.
Classification: LCC QL737.E753 Q38 2020 (print) | LCC QL737.E753 (ebook) | DDC 599.33/2--dc23
LC record available at https://lccn.loc.gov/2019051448
LC ebook record available at https://lccn.loc.gov/2019051449

Photo Credits
AS = Adobe Stock; ASP = Alamy Stock Photo; GI = Getty Images; SS = Shutterstock

Cover, KAMONRAT/SS; top border (throughout), Anvin Iwanicki/SS; vocabulary art (throughout), Linza/AS; 1, JL. Klein & ML. Hubert/Naturagency; 3, kisscsanad/AS; 4, praisaeng/AS; 6, ondrejprosicky/AS; 7 (UP), Oksana Schmidt/GI; 7 (LO), Eyal Bartov/ASP; 8, Mark Thiessen/NGP Staff; 9, Evgeniy/AS; 10, fotoparus/AS; 11, Film Studio Aves/GI; 12-13, fotomaster/AS; 14, Cyril Ruoso/Minden Pictures; 15, Paul Hobson/Nature Picture Library; 16, Anney/AS; 17, Ivan Gaddari/EyeEm/GI; 18, Henrik Larsson/AS; 19, torook/AS; 20 (UP), KAMONRAT/SS; 20 (CTR), vchphoto/AS; 20 (LO), Rico/AS; 21 (UP), imv/GI; 21 (CTR), Vickey Chauhan/SS; 21 (LO), Sergey Kivenko/AS; 22, Alain Le Toquin/Science Source; 23, edward-m/AS; 24-25, jonnysek/AS; 26-27, PerErik/AS; 28-29, Ingo Arndt/Minden Pictures; 30 (LE), nmelnychuk/AS; 30 (RT), jurra8/AS; 31 (UP LE), J. De Meester/Arco Images/ASP; 31 (UP RT), Henrik Larsson/AS; 31 (LO LE), Ingo Arndt/Minden Pictures; 31 (LO RT), Roger Allen Photography/ASP; 32 (UP LE), Anney/AS; 32 (UP RT), Alain Le Toquin/Science Source; 32 (LO LE), Oksana Schmidt/GI; 32 (LO RT), Ivan Gaddari/EyeEm/GI

Table of Contents

What's a Hedgehog?

Is this a porcupine? Or a pinecone with a face?

No—it's a hedgehog!

Hedgehogs are small animals about the size of a guinea (GHIN-ee) pig. They have sharp spines on their head and back.

Where in the World?

Hedgehogs live on the ground in forests, fields, and deserts. They live in many parts of the world.

Hedgehogs live in parts of Africa, Asia, Europe, and the Middle East.

a European hedgehog in a field

This hedgehog lives in the desert in Israel.

7

Sharp Spines

All hedgehogs have spines. Spines are hard, pointy hairs. They keep the hedgehog safe from animals that want to eat it. Foxes, badgers, owls, and hawks hunt hedgehogs.

A hedgehog spine has a sharp end that faces out.

Air pockets inside each spine make the spines light but strong.

When danger is near, a hedgehog curls into a ball. Its face and soft belly stay safe on the inside. The sharp spines stick out on the outside. The spines hurt animals that try to bite the hedgehog.

Parts of a Hedgehog

A hedgehog's body helps it find food and stay safe.

SPINES: Hard spines are made of the same stuff as human hair and nails.

CLAWS: Long claws help dig holes called burrows.

Hedgehog Points

BURROW: A hole dug in the ground that an animal uses as a home

SNOUT: An animal's nose and mouth that stick out from its face

SNOUT: A pointy snout sniffs out food. It pokes under leaves and around bushes and roots.

FUR: Fur covers the face, legs, feet, and belly. It protects the hedgehog's skin.

COLORING: A hedgehog's colors help it hide from animals that want to eat it. Its body blends in with the rocks and bushes around it. Hedgehogs can be brown, white, gray, or tan.

13

Hedgehog Homes

Some hedgehogs live in the country. They live in fields and close to farms.

Other hedgehogs live in cities and towns. They live close to people. They are found in yards, gardens, and city parks.

a hedgehog just
outside its burrow

Some hedgehogs dig a burrow for a home. Others make a nest on the ground with grass and leaves.

During the day, hedgehogs sleep in their homes. At night, they look for food. They are nocturnal (nok-TUR-nul).

Hedgehog Points

NOCTURNAL: Active at night

17

Dinnertime

What is a hedgehog's favorite food? Insects! They also munch on worms, snails, and slugs. Sometimes they eat small mice, spiders, lizards, fruit, and bird eggs.

Hedgehogs eat insects such as beetles.

6 COOL FACTS
About Hedgehogs

1

A hedgehog can have as many as 6,000 spines.

2 Hedgehogs are strong swimmers.

Hedgehogs eat the hard bodies of insects. This helps a hedgehog clean its teeth. **3**

20

The four-toed hedgehog in Africa has four toes on its back feet. All other hedgehogs have five.

Large ears help desert hedgehogs hear well and stay cool. Heat leaves their bodies through the thin skin of their ears.

Hedgehogs grunt and snuffle. They sound like pigs! Some people believe that's how they got the name "hedgehog."

At Rest

Some hedgehogs live in cold places. In the winter, they hibernate (HYE-bur-nate) in nests and burrows.

Hedgehog Points

HIBERNATE: To spend the cold winter months resting. An animal's body slows down when it hibernates.

Long-eared hedgehogs live in hot areas like the desert.

Some hedgehogs live in hot places. They sleep for many weeks during the hot, dry summer. They rest under plants or under the ground.

Hello, Hoglets!

Baby hedgehogs are called hoglets. Most females have four to seven hoglets at one time.

Newborn hoglets are pale pink with short, light-colored spines.

The babies are born with their eyes closed. Their spines are soft and short at first.

The hoglets drink their mother's milk. In a few weeks, their eyes open. They grow new spines that are long and stiff.

Q What do you get when you cross a hedgehog with a cucumber?

A A prickly pickle.

Their mother teaches them to find food. Soon, the hoglets can hunt without her help.

27

Helping Hedgehogs

Hedgehogs are helpful. They eat insects that harm plants. This keeps the plants that feed people and other animals safe.

People can help hedgehogs, too. They can plant bushes and hedges. These make safe places for hedgehogs to live.

People can also help hedgehogs by keeping hollow logs like this in yards and parks. Hollow logs are safe places for hedgehogs to make nests.

What in the World?

These pictures are up-close views of things in a hedgehog's world. Use the hints to figure out what's in the pictures. Answers are on page 31.

1

HINT: These protect a hedgehog.

2

HINT: This body part helps a hedgehog find food.

Word Bank

insect   hoglets   spines   burrow   claws   snout

3

HINT: These are used for digging.

4

HINT: A hedgehog's favorite food

5

HINT: Baby hedgehogs

6

HINT: A hedgehog's home in the ground

Answers: 1. spines, 2. snout, 3. claws, 4. insect, 5. hoglet, 6. burrow

31

BURROW: A hole dug in the ground that an animal uses as a home

HIBERNATE: To spend the cold winter months resting. An animal's body slows down when it hibernates

NOCTURNAL: Active at night

SNOUT: An animal's nose and mouth that stick out from its face

Koalas

Laura Marsh

NATIONAL GEOGRAPHIC

Washington, D.C.

For Elizabeth, Madison, and Kaitlin —L.F.M.

Special thanks to: Deborah Tabart, OAM, CEO of the Australian Koala Foundation; Susan Kelly, Director, Global Briefing; and the Koala Hospital in Port Macquarie, NSW, Australia.

Published by National Geographic Partners, LLC, Washington, DC 20036.

Book design by YAY! Design

Paperback ISBN: 978-1-4263-1466-7
Reinforced library binding ISBN: 978-1-4263-1467-4

Cover (koala), Anna Levan/Shutterstock; 1, Kitch Bain/Shutterstock; 2, Gerry Pearce/Alamy Stock Photo; 4-5, Image100/Jupiter Images/Corbis; 6, Anne Keiser/National Geographic Image Collection; 8, Pete Oxford/Minden Pictures; 9, Yva Momatiuk & John Eastcott/Minden Pictures; 10, Theo Allofs/Minden Pictures; 11, Eric Isselée/Shutterstock; 12, Clearviewimages RM/Alamy Stock Photo; 13, Esther Beaton/Taxi/Getty Images; 14-15, Daniel J Cox/Oxford Scientific RM/Getty Images; 16, Robert Harding World Imagery/Getty Images; 17, surabhi25/Shutterstock; 18 (UP LE), manwithacamera/Alamy Stock Photo; 18 (UP RT), LianeM/Shutterstock; 18 (LO), Flickr RF/Getty Images; 18-19 (Background), Africa Studio/Shutterstock; 19 (UP), Robin Smith/Getty Images; 19 (CTR), Kitch Bain/Shutterstock; 19 (LO), AnthonyRosenberg/iStockphoto; 20 (LE), D. Parer & E. Parer-Cook/Minden Pictures; 20 (RT), Diana Taliun/Shutterstock; 21, Bruce Lichtenberger/Peter Arnold/Getty Images; 22, Flickr RF/Getty Images; 23, shane partridge/Alamy Stock Photo; 24-25, Neil Ennis/Flickr RF/Getty Images; 26, Susan Kelly/Global Briefing/Koala Hospital; 26-27 (Background), Alhovik/Shutterstock; 27 (UP), Joel Sartore/National Geographic Image Collection; 27 (CTR), Susan Kelly/Global Briefing/Koala Hospital; 27 (LO), Joel Sartore/National Geographic Image Collection; 29, Courtesy of Thiess Pty Ltd; 28, Scott E Barbour/Getty Images; 30 (LE), Bruce Lichtenberger/Peter Arnold/Getty Images; 30 (RT), Image100/Jupiter Images/Corbis; 31 (UP LE), Kevin Autret/Shutterstock; 31 (UP RT), Ventura/Shutterstock; 31 (LO LE), Sam Yeh/AFP/Getty Images; 31 (LO RT), roundstripe/Shutterstock; 32 (UP LE), Gerry Ellis/Digital Vision; 32 (UP RT), tratong/Shutterstock; 32 (LO LE), K.A.Willis/Shutterstock; 32 (LO RT), Markus Gann/Shutterstock; Header, arzawen/Shutterstock; Vocab word, Teguh Mujiono/Shutterstock

Table of Contents

Who Am I?

I live in the trees, eating green leaves.

I have a black nose and long claws on my toes.

My big ears are furry. And I'm not in a hurry.

Who am I?
A koala!

Where Koalas Live

PACIFI
OCEAN

Koalas live in a country called
Australia (aw-STRALE-YUH).
They live in forests and wooded
areas. They live in the mountains
and on the coast.

Pouch Animals

Koalas look a little like teddy bears. But they are not bears at all.

Koalas are mammals called marsupials (mar-SOOP-ee-uhls). They carry their babies in pouches. Kangaroos and wombats are marsupials, too.

baby in pouch

wombat

Tree Talk

MAMMAL: An animal that feeds its babies milk. It has a backbone and is warm-blooded.

MARSUPIAL: A mammal that carries its babies in a pouch

kangaroos

Built to Climb

A koala's body is perfect for living in trees.

Its body curls up to fit between branches.

Fur on its bottom is extra thick. It is a built-in seat cushion!

Long arms wrap around trees.

Strong legs help a koala climb up and down trees.

Paws have pads that keep a koala from slipping.

Long claws dig into tree trunks and branches.

Front paws have two thumbs and three fingers. These help grab branches.

Life in the Trees

Koalas are good climbers. They spend most of their time in trees. This is their habitat.

Koalas sleep in trees, too. They doze off in some funny places. Could you sleep like this?

Koalas are slow and sleepy. They sleep up to 18 hours a day.

Tree Talk

HABITAT:
An animal's
natural home

A koala lives in a small area in its habitat. The area has about 100 trees. This is its territory.

Male koalas have a scent patch on their chests. They rub it on the trees.

scent patch

This tells other koalas to stay out of their territory.

Tree Talk

TERRITORY: An area where an animal or group of animals eats, travels, and lives

Picky Eaters

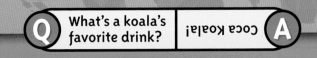
Koalas eat lots of eucalyptus (yoo-ka-LIP-tus) leaves. But they only eat from a few kinds of eucalyptus trees.

To get enough food, koalas eat for about five hours every day. Koalas mostly eat and sleep.

eucalyptus leaves

6 Cool Koala Facts

1

Koalas can jump from tree to tree.

2

Koalas hardly drink any water. They get most of their water from leaves.

3

A koala's fur protects the animal from the heat, cold, and rain.

4

Koalas are very active at night. They like midnight snacks!

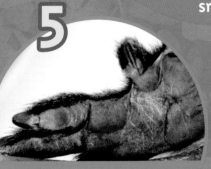

5

Koalas have fingerprints, just like we do.

6

Eucalyptus leaves smell like cough drops. Koalas do, too!

Baby Koalas

A baby koala is called a joey. When it's born, it does not have any hair. It is also blind.

The joey stays in its mother's pouch for about six months. It drinks milk and grows bigger and bigger.

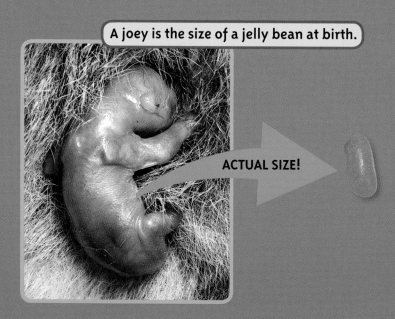

A joey is the size of a jelly bean at birth.

ACTUAL SIZE!

A joey peeks out of mom's pouch.

Soon the joey comes out of the pouch. It hangs on mom's chest or rides on her back.

The young koala learns how to climb and hang on so it can live safely in the trees.

23

In Danger

Today koalas and people often must share space.

Koalas need
land with trees.
But people are
cutting down trees
to make farms,
roads, and buildings.
There is less land
for koalas. They are
in danger.

Koalas get hurt,
too. They get hit
by cars or hurt
by pet dogs.

Helping Koalas

Luckily for koalas, there are hospitals just for them.

Doctors and nurses help koalas that are sick or hurt. Koala hospitals help thousands of koalas every year.

A koala gets help after it was hit by a car. It will be taken to the Koala Hospital in Port Macquarie, New South Wales, in Australia.

This koala's arms were hurt. The casts help them heal.

Hospital workers give loving care to a sick koala.

This koala is being weighed.

Koalas get help in other ways, too. Road signs tell drivers to watch out for koalas.

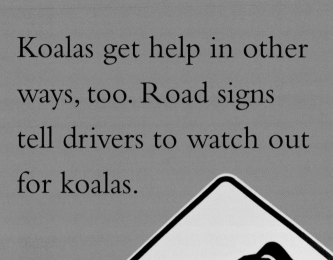

NEXT
10 km

A koala uses a tunnel that goes under a road.

Tunnels and bridges can help koalas cross roads. But koalas don't always know where the safe places to cross are.

Saving eucalyptus trees is the best way to help koalas. Trees are homes for koalas.

What in the World?

These pictures show close-up views of things in a koala's world. Use the hints below to figure out what's in the pictures. Answers on page 31.

HINT: A marsupial carries her baby in here.

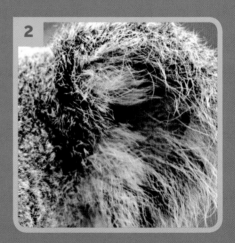

HINT: You have two of these, but they are not furry.

HINT: This is a koala's favorite food.

HINT: These help a koala climb.

HINT: It lives in a pouch after its birth.

HINT: A koala spends almost all of its time here.

Answers: 1. pouch, 2. ears, 3. leaves, 4. claws, 5. joey, 6. trees

HABITAT: An animal's natural home

MAMMAL: An animal that feeds its babies milk. It has a backbone and is warm-blooded.

MARSUPIAL: A mammal that carries its babies in a pouch

TERRITORY: An area where an animal or group of animals eats, travels, and lives

Red Pandas

Laura Marsh

NATIONAL GEOGRAPHIC

Washington, D.C.

For Shelby —L.F.M.

Published by National Geographic Partners, LLC, Washington, DC 20036.

Trade paperback ISBN: 978-1-4263-2121-4
Reinforced library binding ISBN: 978-1-4263-2122-1

Editor: Shelby Alinsky
Art Director: Amanda Larsen
Editorial: Snapdragon Books
Designer: YAY! Design
Photo Editor: Lori Epstein
Production Assistants: Sanjida Rashid and Rachel Kenny
Rights Clearance Specialist: Colm McKeveny
Manufacturing Manager: Rachel Faulise

The author and publisher gratefully acknowledge the expert content review of this book by Brian Williams of the Red Panda Network and the literacy review of this book by Mariam Jean Dreher, professor of reading education at the University of Maryland, College Park.

Illustration Credits

AL = Alamy Stock Photo; NPL = Nature Picture Library; SS = Shutterstock

Cover, Shin Yoshino/Minden Pictures; 1, Juan Carlos Munoz/NPL; 3, Eric Isselée/iStockphoto; 5, Frans Lanting/National Geographic Image Collection; 6, inga spence/AL; 7, Juniors Bildarchiv GmbH/AL; 9, Aaron Ferster/Photo Researchers RM/Getty Images; 10-11, blickwinkel/AL; 12, Krys Bailey/AL; 13, Katherine Feng/Minden Pictures; 14-15, Gary Randall Photography/Kimball Stock; 15, Juan Carlos Munoz/NPL; 16 (UP), Juniors Bildarchiv GmbH/AL; 16 (LO), Paulina Lenting-Smulders/E+/Getty Images; 17 (UP), Jennifer Diehl/Fort Wayne Children's Zoo; 17 (CTR), A & J Visage/AL; 17 (LO), imageBROKER/AL; 18-19, Dr. Axel Gebauer/NPL; 20, Dr. Axel Gebauer/NPL; 21 (UP), WILDLIFE GmbH/AL; 21 (CTR), WILDLIFE GmbH/AL; 21 (LO), WILDLIFE GmbH/AL; 22, JGA/SS; 24-25, Staffan Widstrand/NPL; 26, Dr. Axel Gebauer/NPL; 27, Chris Scharf, Red Panda Network Ambassador; 28 (LE), Chris Scharf, Red Panda Network Ambassador; 28 (RT), csp_sophie_tea/Fotosearch; 29, Cyril Hou/AL; 30 (LE), Jak Wonderly/National Geographic Partners; 30 (RT), Bambax/SS; 31 (UP LE), ang intaravichian/SS; 31 (UP RT), Jak Wonderly/National Geographic Partners; 31 (LO LE), Bildagentur Zoonar GmbH/SS; 31 (LO RT), JGA/SS; 32 (UP LE), Jak Wonderly/National Geographic Partners; 32 (UP RT), Karine Aigner/National Geographic Image Collection; 32 (LO LE), Andy Poole/SS; 32 (LO RT), Chris Godfrey Wildlife Photography/AL; (header throughout), ang intaravichian/SS; (vocab words throughout), Leremy/SS

Table of Contents

Guess Who?

It's the size of a cat.
But it's not that.

It has ears like a bear.
But it's much more rare.

It's out with the moon.
But it's not a raccoon.

Do you need another clue?
Or can you guess who?

It's a red panda!

Many people know about giant pandas. They are big and have black and white fur.

Giant panda

Red pandas share the name "panda." But red pandas and giant pandas are different animals.

A red panda is sometimes called a firefox. Yet a fox and a red panda are not in the same family, either.

Red panda

7

A Forest Home

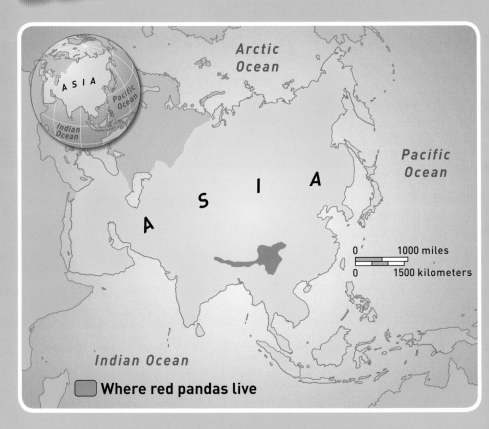

Arctic
Ocean

ASIA

Pacific
Ocean

Indian
Ocean

A S I A

A S I A

Pacific
Ocean

0   1000 miles
0   1500 kilometers

Indian Ocean

Where red pandas live

Red pandas live in mountain
forests in Asia. It gets cold in
the mountains.

So red pandas have thick fur all over. Even the bottoms of their feet have fur. All of this fur keeps them warm.

Life in the Trees

Red pandas are super climbers! They run quickly over branches. A red panda's body helps it live in the trees.

TAIL: A long tail helps it balance on tree branches.

FEET: Fur on the bottoms of its feet keeps it from slipping on wet tree branches.

WRIST BONE: This long bone acts like a thumb. It helps a red panda hang on to branches.

CLAWS: Sharp claws grip the trees while it climbs.

Panda Words

BALANCE: to stay up and not fall over

GRIP: to hold on tightly

Lots of Leaves

Red pandas find food in trees and on the ground. They eat lots and lots of bamboo leaves. They also munch on fruit, grass, and mushrooms.

Bamboo leaves are a favorite food.

Day Sleeper

Red pandas dangle their legs when it's hot.

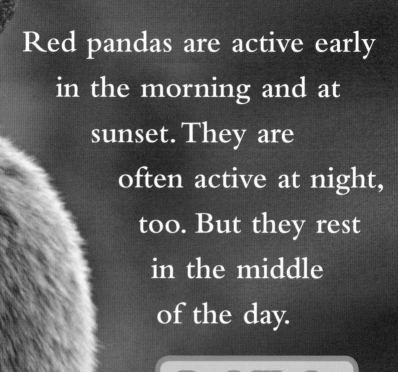

Red pandas are active early in the morning and at sunset. They are often active at night, too. But they rest in the middle of the day.

Panda Word

ACTIVE: likely to move around a lot

They curl up when it's cold.

15

5 FUN FACTS
About Red Pandas

1

Red pandas have very long tails. Their tails are almost as long as their bodies.

2

They lick themselves clean, like a house cat does. This is called grooming.

3 Newborns have hardly any fur on the bottoms of their feet. The fur grows as they get older.

4 In winter, they may spend up to 13 hours a day looking for bamboo and eating it.

5 Red pandas eat about 20,000 bamboo leaves every day.

Little Ones

A mother makes
a nest out of sticks,
leaves, and grass.
She will have her
babies in the nest.

Between one and
four babies will
be born. They are
called cubs.

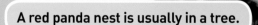

A red panda nest is usually in a tree.

Cubs don't look red when they are born. They are grayish brown. They drink milk and grow bigger. Then their fur turns red.

The mother moves her cub by picking it up in her mouth.

Something to Say

When cubs make
a high whistle
(WISS-ul), their
mom comes running.
It means the cubs
need something—
right now!

Adult red pandas
also make noises.
They may twitter,
squeak, or snort.

Home Area

Red pandas
mostly live alone.
Each red panda
lives in its own
area it calls home.

Sometimes
another red panda
stops by. But it
won't stay for long.

Hide-and-Seek

Can you find the red panda?

Red pandas are shy.
They hide when a predator
(PRED-uh-ter) is near.
They blend in with the forest.
Their black fur matches the
shadows. Their red fur
matches
moss on
the trees.

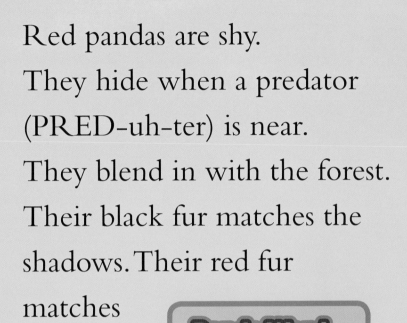

Panda Word

PREDATOR: an animal
that hunts and
eats other animals

Red moss on the trees

We are still learning about red pandas. They are hard to find and study in the wild.

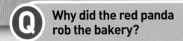

Q Why did the red panda rob the bakery?

A It needed the dough.

People are trying to save the forests where red pandas live. If we save the forests, we can save their homes.

What in the World?

These pictures are up-close views of things in a red panda's world. Use the hints to figure out what's in the pictures. Answers are on page 31.

1

HINT: This part is striped like a raccoon.

2

HINT: Red pandas spend a lot of time here.

Word Bank

nest	claws	tail	leaves	trees	fur

3

HINT: They eat a lot of these.

4

HINT: Red pandas have this all over.

5

HINT: These are used for climbing.

6

HINT: Cubs live here after they are born.

ACTIVE: likely to move around a lot

BALANCE: to stay up and not fall over

GRIP: to hold on tightly

PREDATOR: an animal that hunts and eats other animals

Sea Otters

Laura Marsh

NATIONAL GEOGRAPHIC

Washington, D.C.

For Quintin, Aidan, Gabriel, and Fiona —L.F.M.

The publisher and author gratefully acknowledge the expert review of this book by Andrew Johnson, sea otter research and conservation manager of the Monterey Bay Aquarium.

Published by National Geographic Partners, LLC, Washington, DC 20036.

Book design by YAY! Design

Paperback ISBN: 978-1-4263-1751-4
Library Edition ISBN: 978-1-4263-1752-1

AL = Alamy Stock Photo; GI = Getty Images; NGIC = National Geographic Image Collection; SS = Shutterstock Cover, Kevin Schafer/The Image Bank/GI; 1, Milo Burcham/Superstock; 2, Blaine Harrington III/The Image Bank/GI; 4-5, Mark Newman/The Image Banks/GI; 6 (LO), Tom & Pat Leeson; 6 (UP), Umberto Shtanzman/SS; 7, CORDIER Sylvain/Hemis.fr RM/GI; 8-9, Francois Gohier/VWPics/AL; 10-11, Marvin Dembinsky Photo Associates/AL; 12 (UP LE), altrendo nature/GI; 12 (UP RT), Davies and Starr/The Image Bank/GI; 12 (CTR LE), Colin Keates/Dorling Kindersley/GI; 12 (CTR RT), imagenavi/GI; 12 (LO), Glenn Price/SS; 13, Bipolar/Taxi/GI; 14, Tom & Pat Leeson; 15, Tom & Pat Leeson; 16, Frans Lanting/NGIC; 17, Howard Hall/Blue Planet Archive; 18-19, Kerrick James/GI; 20 (UP), Tom Soucek/AlaskaStock; 20 (LO LE), Doc White/Nature Picture Library; 20 (LO RT), IrinaK/SS; 20-21 (background), SS; 21 (UP LE), YinYang/E+/ GI; 21 (UP RT), Art Wolfe/Science Source; 21 (LO), Morales/age fotostock RM/GI; 22-23, Alaska Stock/AL; 24, Bates Littlehales/NGIC; 25, Doc White/Nature Picture Library; 26-27, Alaska Stock/AL; 27, Marc Moritsch/NGIC; 28, Randy Wilder/Monterey Bay Aquarium; 29, Natalie B. Fobes/NGIC; 30 (RT), C.K.Ma/SS; 30 (LE), Arco Images GmbH/AL; 31 (UP LE), Milo Burcham/SuperStock; 31 (UP RT), Jeff Rotman/Photolibrary RM/GI; 31 (LO LE), Alaska Stock/AL; 31 (LO RT), Kennan Ward; 32 (UP LE), Frans Lanting/NGIC; 32 (UP RT), Jeff Rotman/Photolibrary RM/GI; 32 (LO LE), TonyV3112/SS; 32 (LO RT), M. Shcherbyna/SS; vocab, Destiny VisPro/SS; various (waves vector), Nataleana/SS

Table of Contents

It's a Sea Otter!

What dives and plays
in the water all day?

What floats on its back
when it eats a snack?

What has a flat tail,
but is not a whale?

A sea otter!

What Is a
Sea Otter?

Sea otters are mammals.
They live in the cold Pacific
(puh-SIF-ik) Ocean.

Pacific Ocean

Otter Word

MAMMAL: An animal that feeds its baby milk. It has a backbone and is warm-blooded.

Sometimes sea otters live in zoos or aquariums. They might have been hurt or sick in the wild. Otters get help there.

Otters are fun to watch. They like to play with each other. They dive and splash.

Life in the Sea

Sea otters live close to shore. They find small animals to eat there.

Sea otters dive to the ocean floor. They swim through kelp forests. They need lots of food and clean water to live.

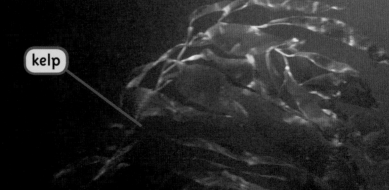

kelp

Q What does an otter say in an emergency?

 A kelp! kelp!

 Otter Word

KELP: A kind of large seaweed that has a long stalk. It can grow into underwater forests.

Built for Hunting

A sea otter's body is perfect for hunting in the water.

TAIL: It helps steer the otter through the water.

BACK LEGS: They are webbed like flippers. They help the otter swim and dive.

FUR: Thick fur keeps the otter warm.

Snack Time

shrimp

scallop

sea urchin

squid

crab

Sea otters eat small animals.
They eat more than 40 different
kinds. They munch on clams, crabs,
squid, urchins, and other animals.
Sea otters have
favorite foods,
just like you.

A sea otter cracks open the shell to eat the animal inside.

Sea otters eat their meals above the water. They lie on their backs. They use their stomachs as plates.

But they don't use a knife and fork! Sea otters use rocks to crack open hard shells.

Scrub-a-Dub!

Do you like to stay clean?
Sea otters do.

They groom themselves for hours
every day. They scrub their faces
and bodies with their paws.

They also somersault (SUM-ur-salt), twist, and turn. This washes food scraps off their bodies. Their fur must stay clean to be warm.

Otter Word

GROOM: To clean by scrubbing, licking, or biting

Fuzzy Fur

It's hard to stay warm in cold water. But a sea otter's fur is up to the job. It is thicker than any other animal's fur.

Q What did the teacher say to the otters causing trouble?

A Go on, get otter here!

The fur has two layers. The outside layer keeps the cold water out. The inside layer stays warm and dry.

6 Cool Facts About Sea Otters

1

Sometimes sea otters hold hands (well, paws)!

2

Sea otters can hold their breath for about five minutes. Most people can't do this for more than one minute.

3

They are members of the weasel family.

4

They eat ten pounds or more of food each day. This gives them energy to swim and hunt.

5

They are the smallest sea mammals in the world.

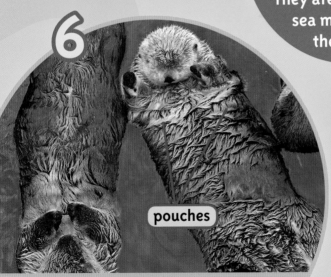

6

pouches

Sea otters have their own pockets. They put food in a pouch under each front leg while hunting.

Playful Pups

A mother otter often floats with her pup on her chest.

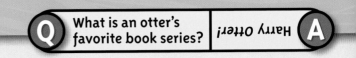

Q What is an otter's favorite book series?

A Harry Otter!

Baby sea otters are born in the water. They are called pups.

Pups are about two feet long at birth. That's about as long as two cereal boxes.

23

The mother teaches her pup how to swim, dive, and roll. But she does the hunting until the pup is older.

A mother may wrap her pup in kelp when she dives. Then the pup will stay in one place while she is away.

Taking It Easy

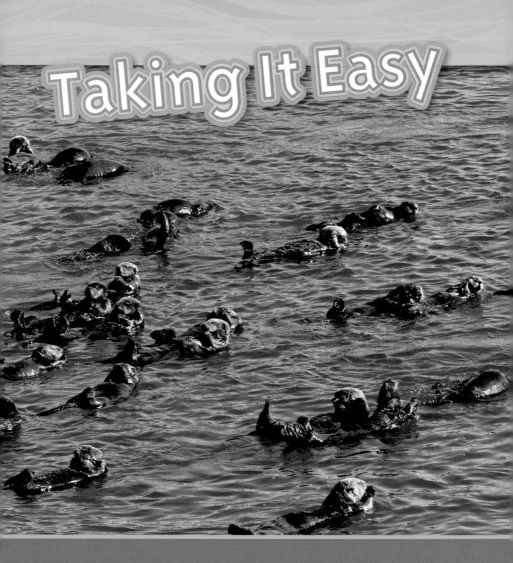

Sea otters live in groups called rafts. The groups are usually all boys or all girls. They spend lots of time together. They rest, groom, and eat.

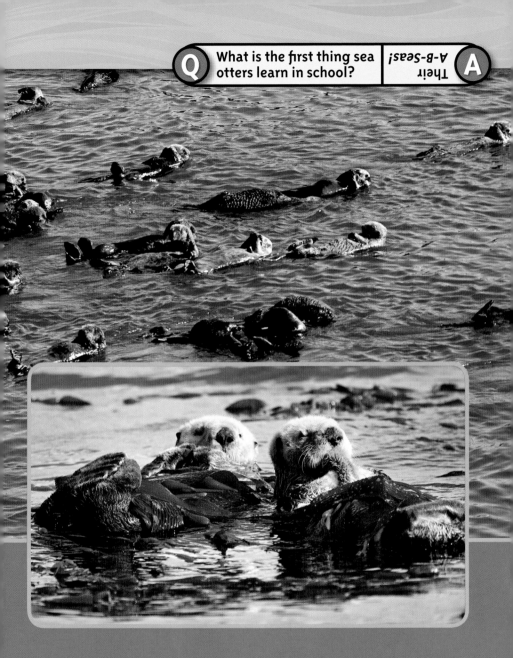

Q What is the first thing sea otters learn in school?

A Their A-B-Seas!

Otters in rafts often wrap themselves in kelp, too. They may sleep like this, side by side.

Watching Out for Otters

Scientists are busy studying sea otters. They want to know how otters live and eat. They want to learn about otters that have gotten sick or hurt, too. Then they can help.

A scientist weighs a sea otter at the Monterey Bay Aquarium.

Scientists do know that pollution (pol-LOO-shun) hurts sea otters. Keeping pollution out of the ocean helps sea otters stay healthy.

Otter Word

POLLUTION: Dangerous material that makes the water, air, or soil dirty

This sea otter was rescued from an oil spill. People helped clean and care for it.

These pictures show close-up views of sea otter things. Use the hints below to figure out what's in the pictures. Answers on page 31.

HINT: An animal that sea otters like to eat

HINT: Sea otters live here.

WORD BANK

| kelp | teeth | paws | squid | fur | ocean |

HINT: This keeps otters warm in cold water.

HINT: A kind of tall seaweed

HINT: These are used to grab food.

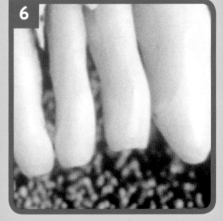

HINT: They tear off bits of food.

Answers: 1. squid, 2. ocean, 3. fur, 4. kelp, 5. paws, 6. teeth

GROOM: To clean by scrubbing, licking, or biting

KELP: A kind of large seaweed that has a long stalk. It can grow into underwater forests.

MAMMAL: An animal that feeds its baby milk. It has a backbone and is warm-blooded.

POLLUTION: Dangerous material that makes the water, air, or soil dirty